SPHYNX CATS

by Mari Schuh

AMICUS HIGH INTEREST • AMICUS INK

Amicus High Interest and Amicus Ink are imprints of Amicus
P.O. Box 1329, Mankato, MN 56002
www.amicuspublishing.us

Library of Congress Cataloging-in-Publication Data
Schuh, Mari C., 1975- author.
 Sphynx cats / by Mari Schuh.
     pages cm. -- (Favorite cat breeds)
 Audience: K to grade 3.
 Summary: "A photo-illustrated book for early readers about the unique hairless Sphynx cats. Describes the Sphynx's unique features, how they were bred to be hairless, their social behaviors, and how they act as pets"-- Provided by publisher.
 Includes index.
 ISBN 978-1-60753-973-5 (library binding)
 ISBN 978-1-68152-102-2 (pbk.)
 ISBN 978-1-68151-007-1 (ebook)
 1. Sphynx cat--Juvenile literature. 2. Cat breeds--Juvenile literature. I. Title.
 SF449.S68S38 2017
 636.8--dc23
                            2015028811

Photo Credits: Vasiliy Koval/Shutterstock cover; IndigoBetta/iStock 2, 9, 14; Alona Rjabceva/iStock 5, 10-11; Lilun_Li/iStock 6; Linn Currie/Shutterstock 13; Oleg Mikhaylov/Shutterstock 16-17; Gerard Lacz Images/Superstock 18; Kekyalyaynen/Shutterstock 21; alkir/iStock 22

Editor: Wendy Dieker
Designer: Tracy Myers
Photo Researcher: Rebecca Bernin

Printed in the United States of America.

HC 10 9 8 7 6 5 4 3 2 1
PB 10 9 8 7 6 5 4 3 2 1

TABLE OF CONTENTS

Unique and Rare   4

History   7

Hairless Cats   8

Wrinkly Skin   11

Grooming   12

Big and Long   15

Friendly Cats   16

Full of Energy   19

Family Pets   20

How Do You Know It's a Sphynx?   22

Words to Know   23

Learn More   24

Index   24

UNIQUE AND RARE

A bald cat walks in the sun. The sun warms its skin. The cat does not look like other cats. It is **unique**. And there are not very many of them. The cat is a Sphynx.

HISTORY

The Sphynx is a new cat breed. In 1966, a cat gave birth to a hairless kitten. The owner found other people with hairless cats. These cats soon had kittens with no fur.

HAIRLESS CATS

A Sphynx only looks like it has no hair. It actually has soft **down**. The down is short, fuzzy hair. It is hard to see. The cat's skin feels like a peach.

Fun Fact
A Sphynx's skin can be different colors and patterns.

WRINKLY SKIN

Sphynx cats have soft, warm skin. Their skin has **wrinkles**. Other cats have wrinkles too. But the wrinkles are under their fur. We can't see them.

GROOMING

A Sphynx's skin can be oily. The cats clean themselves. But they also need a weekly bath. Their ears need to be cleaned too.

Like a Wild Cat?

Sphynx cats lick their bodies to stay clean. So do cougars and tigers in the wild.

13

BIG AND LONG

Sphynx cats have big ears. Their ears look like bat ears. These cats have big eyes. They have long toes. Sphynx cats have big, round bellies. Their tails are long.

Like a Wild Cat?

Some Sphynx have tails that look like a lion's tail. Their tails have a puff of hair on the end.

FRIENDLY CATS

Sphynx cats like to be with people. They follow their owners. They also greet visitors. Sphynx snuggle to stay warm. They are friendly cats.

Fun Fact
A Sphynx often wags its tail when it is around people.

FULL OF ENERGY

Sphynx are **curious**. They explore and play. They climb and leap like a monkey. These cats have lots of energy.

FAMILY PETS

Sphynx are smart and loving. They get along with kids and other pets. Sphynx cats look different than other cats. But they make great pets.

HOW DO YOU KNOW IT'S A SPHYNX?

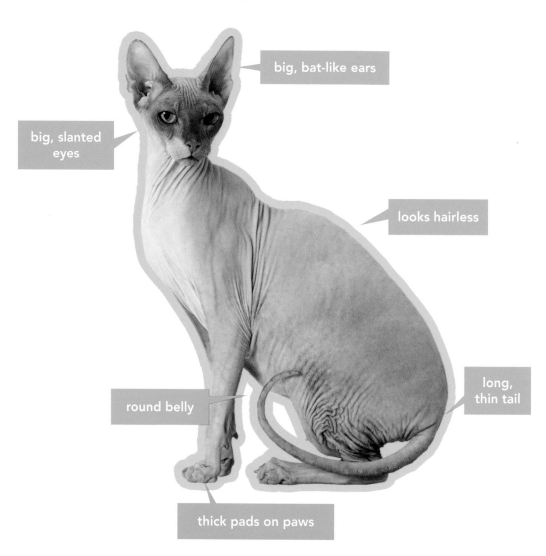

big, bat-like ears

big, slanted eyes

looks hairless

long, thin tail

round belly

thick pads on paws

WORDS TO KNOW

breed – a type of cat

curious – eager to learn and find out about new things

down – fine, soft hair

unique – one of a kind

wrinkles – folds or lines on the skin

LEARN MORE

Books
Felix, Rebecca. *Sphynx Cats.* Cool Cats. Minneapolis: Bellwether Media, 2016.

Owen, Ruth. *Sphynx.* Cats Are Cool. New York: PowerKids Press, 2014.

Websites
Cat Fanciers' Association: For Kids
http://kids.cfa.org/index.html

Discovery Kids: Top Cats
http://discoverykids.com/articles/top-cats/

INDEX

baths 12

ears 15

friendly 16

hair 8

kittens 7

pets 20
playing 19

rare 4

skin 8, 11, 12

tail 15, 16

wrinkles 11

29.93